SLAVERY:

Its Sin, Moral Effects, and Certain Death.

ALSO

THE LANGUAGE OF NATURE,

Compared with Divine Revelation,

IN PROSE AND VERSE.

'Tis Heaven's decree, "Slavery must die,"
Freedom to all! is proclaimed from on high.

BY JUSTUS KEEFER.

WITH EXTRACTS FROM EMINENT AUTHORS.

BALTIMORE:
J. KEEFER, PUBLISHER,
No. 109 N. BROADWAY.

Liberty, with one mighty stroke,
Proclaims Ethiopia free!
And shouts the death of Slavery.

SLAVERY.

I.

When wars are raging, who can speak
  Of a country's weal or woe?
When nations grow too proud or great,
  And their God refuse to know,
He'll surely break their idols,
  And their temples overthrow;
But the Patriot, the noble and brave,
Made *morally fit* his country to save,
May sheathe the sword, for victory is sure,
When the heart that strikes for freedom is pure;.

But enough! 'tis not of a nation's quarrel
My muse would write; so, preferring the moral—
To seek out the wrong, and it pursue—
I turn, oppressed Africa, to you.

II.

Long have you borne the heavy burden,
But now your prayers are heard in heaven;
Let angels the glorious news proclaim,
Africa's free! and her sons God's free men!

III.

Instead of chains and hopeless tears,
The master's lash and threatening fears;
The auctioneer's boisterous jest,
As he tears from the mother's breast
Her babe, her hope, her life, her all,
Hushing with stripes her frantic call:
Instead of these—O, glorious hope!
Liberty, with one mighty stroke,
Proclaims Ethiopia free,
And shouts the death of Slavery!

IV.

The thunder of war, rolling o'er the plains,
Declares the truth that men, though in chains,
  Are born equal and free.
Thy tears, fond mother, were not shed in vain;
They were bottled in heaven, and now they rain
  Blessings on thy race and thee.

V.

Heaven slumbers not, and her judgments are sure;
The cries of thy babe on a far-distant shore,
  (Though in vain, to see thy face,)
Are heard in heaven in behalf of thee,
And to thy poor, oppressed posterity,
  Bring joy and heavenly grace.

VI.

Hark! O Christian mother! turn not away
From that voice of wailing and sad misery;
Think, when at even you retire to rest,
(Your babe nestling sweetly upon your breast,)
Of that mother doomed to slavery and chains;

No time to improve either body or brains!
Does not your tender heart in horror recoil
At such scenes of oppression and ceaseless toil?

VII.

God has endowed her with feelings, e'en as thee;
Placed within her breast the germ of Liberty;
Given her a mind — aye, and reason as well,
That she might as fondly her little ones tell
Of a Father's love, a home beyond the skies,
Where tyrant masters no longer mock their cries.
Slave mother! may your heart to him be given
Who died for all, and ope'd for all a heaven—
An everlasting rest, where God's impartial grace,
According to the heart, appoints each one his place.

VIII.

Thou enemy of Freedom, gaze upon that babe
Of innocence — heaven's chosen type;
What horror would fill your soul if some one had said
This child's not yours, and even this very night
The law claims its own! *Is the law right?*

IX.

Then teach that child, before its lisping tongue—
Or ere its organ of speech
Can pronounce that word of infinite wrong—
O, mother! in heaven's name, teach
Through this medium the ages to come,
That of all the evils under the sun,
That most allied—*and 'tis the truth you know*—
That most allied to the regions of woe,
And that, too, in the lowest degree,
Is this crimson-dyed sin—*Slavery*.

X.

Now hear, O ye favored! ye who'd be truly great:
'Tis not by being masters, but humble and meek;
'Tis not your person, nor the color of your skin,
That God respects, but truth and righteousness within.
All else, then, being equal, he loves you no more
Than the poor unlettered slave who waits at your door.
Whether Jew or Gentile, bond or free,
In Christ all are one. *So may it be.*

XI.

My sin-sick soul, weary and oppressed,
  Craves some quiet haunt that man can't degrade;
A retreat in "some vast wilderness,
  Or boundless continuity of shade,"
Where oppression could never reach me more,
Nor sin polute that quiet, peaceful shore.

XII.

My ear is pained with ev'ry day's report
  Of the wrongs of which the earth is filled,
Which cause the blood in man's obdurate heart
  To stiffen with a convulsive chill!
My restless soul looks abroad, but in vain,
For that natural bond and love among men;
For the one being weak and the other strong,
(Thus having the power to enforce a wrong)—
Blush, O humanity! when I say—
Dooms and devotes him his lawful prey.

XIII.

Thus man dooms his fellow—exacts the sweat of him
  Created in the moral image of his God;

And, as if 'twere not enough, O, monstrous sin!
Lays stripes upon his back, thus forcing his blood
In a way that, were it inflicted on a beast,
Mercy, with a bleeding heart, would hang her head
and weep.

XIV.

Then what, alas! is man, or what man, seeing this,
(His brother held like a beast by a chain,)
That would not hang his head and in confusion blush
To feel, to think, to own himself a man!

XV.

Yes, man destroys his brother; and O! is it not,
Of all human miseries, the most to be deplored!
Upon the pages of sin, 'tis the foulest blot,
And, of all others, the most to be abhorred.

XVI.

I'd not have a slave to till my ground,
Or fan me while I sleep;
To tremble at each disturbing sound,
And tremble when I wake,

For all the wealth of sinews bought and sold;
For this would be ill-gotten, sordid gold!

XVII.

No! dear and sacred as Freedom is,
  And, in my estimation, prized above all price,
I had rather myself be the slave,
  Than doom a brother an unwilling sacrifice.

XVIII.

O! shame, then, that man, the noblest work of God,
With high and holy aspirations endowed,
Who, blest with a nature to feel and believe
It infinitely better to give than receive;
A nature that seeks to comfort the oppressed
With a spirit of disinterestedness,
That *he* should engage in acts so foul—
Acts that degrade and corrupt the soul!

XIX.

Those finer feelings that adorn the soul,
Have been corrupted by a thirst for gold.

With ears that won't hear, and eyes that won't see,
And a heart that won't feel another's misery,
Man grinds the face of God's suffering poor,
'Til a broken heart, that can bear no more,
Dies a victim to this monster; and what is still worse,
Incapable of pity or feelings of remorse.

XX.

Why should man thus despise his fellow-man,
If nature clothes him with a darker skin?
Tis a vain cause, surely, for wicked strife;
For of the heart are the issues of life;
From this the all-seeing eye of God
Writes a true and impartial record;
If the heart be right 'tis well, for then
Art thou only accepted of him;
Whether white or black, bond or free,
Race, or color, argues nothing for thee.

XXI.

All flesh is mine, says the eternal God,
And surely I'll exact every man's blood;

At his hands will I exact it again,
Who holds his brother in slavery and sin;
Then hear, O ye nations! heaven's decree—
Tis God that speaks—Let my people go free!

XXII.

A great work for humanity's come:
'Tis heard in the cannon's loud roar;
'Tis heard in each tap of the drum,
In the rolling thunders of war;
It is seen upon the battle-field,
Where God's armies cover the plain—
Reflected from each warrior's shield,
Each sabre, glitt'ring in the sun;
The bugle, as it calls to arms,
To the friends of Freedom proclaims,
The year of jubilee has come.

XXIII.

Yes, the year of jubilee has come;
O Ethiopia! to thee
Each sigh, each tear, each stripe, each groan,

Strikes a death blow to Slavery!
And your soldiers brave the shout will raise, We are free!
Inscribe on their banners, Life, Hope and Liberty.

XXIV.

Thus Liberty greets thee, as with waving hands
She bids thee onward to the field;
There is hope in her smile, and in her commands
All tyrants shall be made to feel
That now 'tis thy turn to deal back the blow
Their pitiless hearts so oft did bestow;
With shame and reproach, e'en from thee they shall learn,
As we do to others we receive in return.

XXV.

Then arise! away with these galling chains!
Let Ethiopia forget her pains;
The avenger of tyranny and wrong
Will lead thee to victory; then onward, on!
Yes, God will avenge his suffering poor,
E'en though by the scourge and horrors of war!

XXVI.

The type of thy freedom is in the slave,
Marching boldly to battle with the brave;
Then onward with a firm and steady step,
If honest and true, you'll never regret;
A pure heart, and conscience void of offense,
Is the best guide at the smallest expense.
Then, when the enemy appears in view,
Be calm: strike with a firm and steady blow;
Raise the battle-cry—"*Freedom! Liberty!*—
Death to tyrants, traitors and Slavery!"

XXVII.

Forget not the wrongs, outrage and disgrace,
Endured so long by your oppressed race;
Let your ears be deaf to every sound save
Those which issue from the deep-vaulted grave!
The groans and cries of a father, a mother,
Or, perchance, thine own child, sister or brother:
"Avenge our blood," you should still hear them say,
Though their bodies lie mould'ring in the clay.

XXVIII.

But see that you follow where God doth lead;
Let no selfish vengeance your passions feed.
"Vengeance is mine; I'll repay," saith the Lord;
So prosper you must, if you heed his word.
Surely thou art *honored* in bearing arms,
And this to thy race should have many charms.
Then grasp the sword firmly—challenge the fight;
It leads the way to equity and right.

XXIX.

As an instrument in the hands of God,
You will have to bear a less heavy load.
A slave! a soldier! Who cannot discern
The contrast? and with a heart that must burn
For Freedom—Freedom for himself and race—
Nothing less can remove this foul disgrace.

XXX.

Then let the scabbard hang empty by
The side of him who had rather die
Than be a slave!—yes, there let it hang,

And let not the sword return again
Until Freedom, although dearly bought,
Be the boon of those brave souls who fought,
'Til *treason* is crushed, and our nation see
The dawn of universal Liberty!

XXXI.

"Cry aloud and spare not, and be sure you proclaim
To my people and the house of Jacob their sin.
They seek me daily, and delight to know my ways;
A nation that did right, e'en as in other days;
Forsook not the ord'nance nor oracles of God,
They ask of me justice and delight in my word.
Wherefore have we fasted? say they in surprise,
And thou behold'st not, nor see'st with thine eyes?
We afflict our souls, and thou takest no knowledge;
Wherefore do we labor and have no advantage?"

XXXII.

"Behold, ye fast for strife;" ye quarrel and debate;
Smite with the fist of wickedness, envy and hate;

But ye shall not so fast as ye do this day,
To make your voice heard with railing on high.
Is it such a fast I have chosen? Nay, behold!
'Tis not my will that man should thus afflict his soul,
To bow down his head and appear as a bulrush;
To cover it with ashes and mourn in sackcloth.
"Behold! is not this the fast that I have chosen:
To loose the wicked bands and the heavy burden?
Is it not to deal thy bread to the poor, and see
Every yoke broken, and that the oppressed go free?

XXXIII.

Come, then, to the work, O ye men of God!
And boldly proclaim his blessed word;
Let not the organ of moral reform
Withhold its strong and powerful arm.
Why be so fearful lest ye give offense,
Be charged with over zeal or imprudence?
What though the people should rise up and say,
"He preaches politics!" and then go away?

XXXIV.

Be not discouraged, if but twelve remain,
'Twas even so in the great Master's time.
The truth is not always pleasing, you know,
But persevere—it is destined to grow.
Compromise it not, neither hold your peace;
Sow the seed, and God will give the increase.

XXXV.

Light with darkness can never agree;
And so with Freedom and Slavery.
Truth in one and error in another,
Create strife between brother and brother.
"I come not to send peace but a sword!"
And, as in the days of our blessed Lord,
So now. Christ with Baal cannot agree,
Nor with the spirit of Slavery.

XXXVI.

"Behold!" men say, "an evil hath been,"
And so justify the present sin.

"Come," say they, "let us oppress the poor,
The same as our father's did of yore!"
Thus they rebel and fight against God,
And stain their hands in innocent blood.

XXXVII.

Shall this thing be, and you hold your peace?
Shall the threatenings of God's law thus cease?
Shall the wicked mock, make light of sin,
And you remain passive lookers on?
Nay! proclaim the doctrine of my word,
And "stand in my counsel," saith the Lord,
"That you may cause my people to fear,
And save both thyself and them that hear."

XXXVIII.

"Hear, O king of Judea!" thus saith the Lord,
"Speak to thy servants, thy people, my word."
Thou that sittest on David's throne, proclaim
That they cease from evil and do no wrong
To the stranger, the widow, the fatherless,

But execute judgment in righteousness,
For he that buildeth his chambers by wrong,
Withholding wages for services done,
Shall not do so this day, but give
To ev'ry one his wages, and live!

XXXIX.

So preach, O ye who stand on Zion's hill!
Blow loud the gospel trumpet, e'en until
All—yes, until the poor bondsman shall know
The great salvation which through Christ doth flow.

XL.

Had I a voice that could reach all round
This Globe, with thrill and piercing sound,
With one loud blast I'd summons all men
To hearken—and this should be my theme—
Rise, O ye people! rise in your strength,
Throughout the land, its breadth and its length
And, with one united stroke, for ever slay
This hydra-headed monster—*Slavery*.

XLI.

Mark ye well the man—nay, that vile thing
Who'd be guilty of so foul a sin,
To put a chain round his brother's neck,
And make of human blood a traffic.
Of all the race this man is the one
That humanity should blush to own

XLII.

"Perpetual slavery!" I loathe the sound!
This ceaseless toil—this one continued round
Of work. This night of sorrow knows no day;
Not one cheering hope; not a single ray
Of light to chase away this dismal gloom—
Worse, far worse than the darkness of the tomb.

XLIII.

And for what? What *evil* has he done,
That the father, his child, and so on,
Until *all*—e'en the entire race—
Must yield to this infamous disgrace.

XLIV.

The light of God's truth can scarce reach the soul
In this dreary waste, so dismal and cold;
Here the mind, untutored and untaught,
Lies withering and incapable of thought.

XLV.

O, ye who bear the Christain name,
Look on your slave, and O, for shame!
Since righteous you profess to be,
Undo these chains—this misery!
Thy slave has a soul e'en as thou,
And in Christ all are free, you know.
By what moral right, then, can ye hold
His subjects under your control?

XLVI.

Will ye say, by the right of power,
The same as in the days of old?
Ah! what scenes of bloodshed and war
Are practiced now by this same rule!

Ye quote the Scriptures and insist
That these to Slavery do hold,
But other evils—not only this,
Were practiced in those times, we're told:
They speak of Noah's fondness for wine,
And the incest of good old Lot;
The concubinage of Abraham,
And the polygamy of Jacob.
Why not conclude that these are no sin,
Since all were practiced, we see, by them?

XLVII.

Ah! ye thirst for gold, and the mind would have ease;
Hence ye seek in the Bible for excuse,
With little effort the heart is made believe
That always right which suits the present use.
Thus you bring reproach upon God's blessed word,
Force the Scriptures to teach that which is untrue;
But ye friends of Slavery, thus saith the Lord,
"Do to others as you'd have others do to you."

XLVIII.

Slavery, as a penalty for sin,
Was allowed, but with a woe unto him
Who, without limit of time or mercy,
Would dare exact his sweat or usury.
But truth is progressive, and this we know,
That nations do wiser and better grow;
For the time has been, (O how sad to believe,)
When Christian baptism was refused the slave!

XLIX.

Now the reason for this is plain to see;
Baptized into Christ, they all become free.
Then shout the truth, ye ages, as ye roll on:
There is Liberty for all in God's dear son.

L.

Thus, by virtue of redeeming grace,
The right of property in human flesh
Is null; and this, as none can fail to see,
Is bad news to the friends of Slavery.

LI.

Thus, fearing your craft would come to nought,
(And what soul does not sicken at the thought?)
Man, created with an immortal mind,
Is doomed to ignorance of the grossest kind;
He must not read nor instructed be,
For knowledge inclines to Liberty.

LII.

What man, having the feelings of a man,
That would not hang his head and blush for shame,
To own a system so corrupt as this,
That puts man on a level with a beast?

LIII.

The Scriptures do teach, "Let your light shine."
"Not so," proclaims some modern divine,
"Our system must by ignorance live;
So darkness—not light—suits best the slave."

LIV.

O thou—to say the least—misguided man!
Sooner or later you will understand

That *mind* cannot be holden with a chain;
It will break its fetters and rise again.
Your system of oppression may last for a while,
But God will hear the cries of his suffering child.

LV.

"Go through the land, preach my gospel to all;"
Is not this your ministerial call?
For how can they hear without a preacher,
Or the ignorant learn without a teacher?
Faith comes, you know, by hearing God's word;
But how shall they believe who never heard?

LVI.

Should you preach to your slave, what would you say?
That the wife should the husband obey?
That the husband should love and cherish his wife,
And make her the object of his care through life?
Would you say, furthermore, that they twain were one—
United never again to be undone?

Nay; you'd scarce be guilty of such a blunder,
To say they should never be put asunder;
For well do you know that ere another day,
A mortgage on his life might tear him away.

LVII.

Ah! 'twere but mockery and foul deceit;
For the slave, you must know, has not the right
To succor his offspring, protect his wife;
To defend either theirs or his own life.
They are not his, save by moral right,
Which a legal process can abrogate.
Thus a mere chattel, like his master's ox, or horse,
He is whipt or sold without pity or remore.

LVIII.

The marriage rite—heaven's sacred gift to man—
Ye deny, and with a high and wicked hand,
Remove and erase it from the word of God,
Thus changing and corrupting his blessed word;
But to them that add to or take therefrom,
Shall be added the plagues written therein.

LIX.

My sick and weary soul doth mourn
That love which seeketh not her own,
But another's good.
O when will man—vain, selfish man—
This lesson rightly understand,
And spread its fruits abroad?

LX.

Spread abroad a knowledge of God;
His universal Fatherhood,
And man's own destiny.
Teach the slave to worship and pray,
Nor wear his precious soul away
In chains and slavery.

LXI.

A lifetime of toil to undergo,
Is surely too much misery and woe,
E'en for the Father;
But his innocent child, pure as the morn,

Alas! too soon the same hard fate must learn,
And that from a brother.

LXII.

O slavery! thou curse of the vilest breed!
Not only in the world dost sow thy seed;
For, strange to discover,
Those who, by Christian profession, seek
To comfort the poor and protect the weak,
Oppress one another.

LXIII.

But God has set a furnace in the earth;
Its flames the cannon are now belching forth.
These thunders will not cease to roll,
(Though the earth vibrate from pole to pole,)
'Til the sin-laden clouds have ceased to rain,
And the moral atmosphere is pure again.

LXIV.

Then this night of sorrow will flee away
Before the dawn of a glorious day;

Again the morning stars will sing for joy,
And righteousness become each soul's employ;
For a new creation, new heavens and new earth,
From his fiery furnace God will bring forth;
Then let the nation's bow—the Lord doth reign—
And every soul shout, "*Amen! Amen!*"

SLAVERY.

We take great pleasure in adding the following from the pen of the Rev. J. D. Paxton:

"There are many things in negro slavery, as it exists among us, to which we all would think it exceedingly hard and unjust, to be ourselves and families subjected. Now the law of "doing as we would be done by"—the law of "loving our neighbor as ourselves,"—appears to me most manifestly to forbid that we should subject others to these things.

The negro slave may, with a solitary exception, be said to be stript of all his rights. The law recognizes his right to life, and makes some provisions to secure it from being violently taken away; but even those provisions are far short of what are deemed necessary to secure the life of the white man. How this difference is viewed in the eyes of him who "made of one blood all nations of men," and declares "himself no respector of persons," deserves the serious consideration of all, and especially of those who call God their Father, and profess to take his word for the rule of their conduct.

With the above exception, I hardly know the right, natural, civil or religious, which the slave can be said to possess. All are claimed by the master; and the law of the land sustains his claim. The slave is reduced to a mere chattel—is held by his master as property, with absolute and uncontrolled authority to use him and treat him as his interest, or passion, or caprice may dictate. The slave may be bought and sold at pleasure, and that without any regard to his inclinations; without any regard to long and faithful services, and without any regard to family ties. His times of labour and of rest, the kind and degree of labor, depend on the will of his master. Should a master refuse the degree of rest needful to support nature—should he work his slave beyond his natural strength—the slave has no redress. No one is authorized to interfere. The master claims the whole proceeds of the labor of the slave, and that without acknowledging any obligation to give any compensation, more than a bare subsistence. And as to the means of subsistence, the kind and quantity of food and clothing, the master has it absolutely in his power. Should he give what is unhealthy in kind and insufficient in quantity, there is no redress. The master may punish his slave in what manner and degree he pleases, (not immediately taking life,) for his faults, real or suspected, or for no fault at all. Should a master from prejudice, or caprice, or sheer cruelty, abuse and punish and torture his slave every day, as much as his nature would bear, I know of no law of the land which would make it the duty or enable any one to interfere and stop the crying injustice. The master may cut off his slave to what extent he please from intercourse with the world. He may prevent his forming family connections, or he may break them up when formed. Where the relation of husband and wife exists in good faith between the parties, and is strengthened by all the endearments of a family of children, the pledges of their mutual love, the law still gives no protection. The master may sell the husband without the wife, or the wife without the husband; the parents without the children, or the children without the parents. He may sell them all—he may sell them all separately—one to one man, to be removed in one direction, and another to another man, to be taken in a different direction, as his interest, passion or caprice may influence. The owner may keep his slaves as ignorant as he please, or as ignorant as he can. He may refuse to teach them to read, and may forbid any other person to do it; he may oppose their religious instruction; He may prevent their attending the preaching of the Gospel; he may place them in situations so remote from the public means of grace, and so lay his commands on them as to staying at home, that, humanly speaking, the slave has no chance of hearing and understanding the gospel to his salvation. Yea, so absolute is the power of the master, and so cut off from all help and all defence is the slave, that the slave may be obliged to enter on and pursue sinful courses. Female slaves may be compelled to unclean living. The direct power of the owner or manager to enforce his wishes by hard usage and punishment in various forms, and the want of means and defence on the part of the slave, even as to giving testimony against a white man, places the purity of the female, and the comfort and happiness of both male and female, as connected with female purity and mutual confidence, in the power of those over them. Whether slaves be allowed to perform parental duties, educate their children, or children perform filial duties, depends on the will of the owner.

It would be easy to add to the above statement other things in which the situation of the slave is most exposed—is most hard—is such as their masters would be utterly unwilling to be held in themselves with their families — is such that masters would think it righteous in the sight of God and man to run every hazard and contend even unto blood, rather than continue in it, and leave it a heritage of sufferings and wrongs to their children.

Now the single question I would press for an answer, given in the fear of God, is this:

Is the believer in the Bible, is the professor of the religion of Christ, justified — can he be justified in the sight of him who is no respecter of person? — Can he be justified by that word of God which commands him to "love his neighbor as himself?" — by that command of Christ, "In all things whatsoever ye would that men should do unto you, do ye even so to them," can he, I say, be justified in holding a fellow creature deprived of his rights which, in his own case, he declares unalienable; and for which he would think himself justified in the sight of heaven and earth, in contending even unto blood? — Can he be justified in giving his countenance to a system, which is based on a total disregard for rights, which he puts in the same scale with his own existence,—a system which opens the door for evils and oppressions, against which he would think it right to defend himself and family at every hazard? Can he be acquitted before that "God who is of purer eyes that to behold iniquity," in giving in to a practice pregnant with so many evils; which presents such strong temptations to iniquity, and which operates in so many ways against the salvation of both master and slaves?

I think it useless here to enumerate all the ways in which professors of religion explain the "rule of doing as we would be done by," in its application to slavery. Perhaps the more common way is to apply the rule to the case in a very partial manner; in a manner so partial as not at all to touch its most essential parts. Thus the whole matter of depriving a fellow creature of his rights, or (which in its morality is the same) withholding them from him, is passed over.

The rule of doing as we would be done by is not applied to the act of withholding his rights, but to the treatment he receives, considered as thus stripped of them! We daily meet with persons who appear to make the whole morality of holding slaves consist in the manner of treating them. To the treatment of slaves simply considered, they, in some sort, apply the rule; but to the act of holding a fellow creature in slavery, considered separately from his treatment in that state, they appear not to apply the rule at all. They take it for granted that the "rule of doing as we would be done by," allows the holding of slaves, provided we treat them well.

Now this to me appears, most manifestly, a partial application of the rule to the case. The most important part of the case is not tried by the rule at all. No question is made about stripping a fellow creature of rights, or withholding them from him. And why not? Is it not one of those cases in which we can suppose ourselves in a change of place, and so apply the rule as easily as we can to any special act of treatment towards those in slavery? On what authority is it withdrawn from the catalogue, embraced by our

Savior in the first part of his rule: "In all things, &c., do ye, &c."

It appears to me capable, if not of absolute demonstration, yet of a high degree of proof, that the single act of withholding from a fellow creature his rights, or, in other words, the holding him in slavery, is the "very head and front of the offending." This is the great original sin in every case where slavery, such as exists among us, is found. The treatment of slaves may be good or bad, kind or cruel, in all their various degrees; and may of course be more or less conformable to the "rule of doing as we would be done by." But the act of depriving a fellow creature of his rights to the extent the negro slave is deprived of his, or the act of withholding or refusing to restore them; or, in other words, the act of holding him in slavery,—is at all times and in all situations a violation of the rule. For plainly, no man who has common sense and understands the case would be willing to be stripped of his rights and held in slavery such as the negro is doomed to. So far from being will ing to be treated thus, he would think it most hard; he would, if he understood his natural rights as most masters do, think it most unrighteous; and would think it right to make every effort to burst the bands and go out free. Now on what principle is it that the rule "of doing as we would be done by" is not applied to this case? May the professor of religion in the face of the rule and in the hearing of the declaration of his Master, "with what measure ye mete, it shall be measured to you again,"—mete out the hard measure of slavery to a fellow creature, while he would at every hazard refuse it in his own case?

I pass by for the present all the questions respecting the treatment of slaves, and the bearing it may have on their opinions on this subject. For the sake of getting that part of the question separated from the other, let us suppose that they are treated as well as they ought to be—that the law of doing as we would be done by, applied fairly to the case of their treatment, finds no fault; still he is in slavery, and what is implied in that? Why he is stripped of all his rights; is entirely under the power of another; is held as property with a long train of disabilities and deprivations, and liabilities to evils and oppressions in all their varieties. Now the question returns, do the laws which Christ has given his people to regulate their conduct towards their fellow men, allow of this stripping another of his rights, or withholding them from him? It appears to me most manifest that they do not, and yet many appear to see the matter differently. It seems, therefore, necessary to attempt a farther illustration of it.

No injuries are more pernicious to us, no injustice is more cruel than that done to our rights. This surely needs no proof in the day in which we live, and among the free and enlightened people of America. Injuries of no other kind are to be compared with them. The reason is plain. While we are invested with our rights, they are our armor of defence against all kinds of evils to which we are exposed from our fellow men, and where an injury is received our rights in their legitimate operation will procure us amends. They are an armor defensive and offensive. They afford security. But where, in any case, they fail to do that, they enable us to procure amends for the evil suffered.

But suppose we are injured in our just unalienable rights; suppose we are stripped of them; suppose they are forcibly withheld from us, our armor of defence is gone. We may be injured every day—we may be assailed on every part. We have no help. We have not the means of defending ourselves against the injury; we have not the means of getting amends for it.

To illustrate this case, suppose a man or a body of men deprived of the single right of self-defence, and that not for any crime, but to enable those who deprived them of the right to accomplish certain purposes with them, their families, property, &c., the fact that some of these persons might, owing to peculiar circumstances, feel but little inconvenience from the cruel measure, would not alter the character of the measure, nor lessen the guilt of those who passed it. The very nature and tendency of the measure was to expose them to oppression, injury, and wrong, and that without redress. No one act of wrong that they might meet with under it, nor any number of acts would equal, in their amount of wrong, the injustice and cruelty of the single act which stripped them of the right of self-defence, and for the plain, simple reason that the act which stripped them of the right of self-defence, exposed them to all kinds of assaults and injuries from all sorts of persons at all times and places.

Or suppose any man or body of men put out of the protection of the law, not for any crime, but simply that those who did it might treat them as they please and serve themselves of them. To what does not their outlawry expose them? They may be watched and waylaid, and ensnared; they may be hunted with men, and guns, and dogs, and all kinds of offensive weapons; they may be deceived and betrayed by acquaintances, relations and friends. No person, no place nor time is so sacred as to afford protection.

Now it would take nothing from the monstrous injustice of the outlawry, were we to suppose that some of the outlawed, owing to peculiar circumstances, felt few, if any, of these evils, and for the obvious reason that the act of outlawry exposed to all sorts of evils. It was its nature to do this, and if they all did not fall on the victim, no thanks to the act, nor to those who passed it. The act of outlawry is the great injury—the original sin in the case. More or less evil may flow from it, as times and other things may permit; but it produces no good of itself, but evil, only evil, and that continually.

That injuries in our rights are the greatest evils we are exposed to—are great mother-evils, which are prolific of others to an unknown extent—is well understood by the American people. This is evidenced by the fact that both the wars which were carried on against England were for rights.

The special act of injury committed at the commencement of the revolutionary war, considered separately from the rights involved, would, we may safely say, not have produced war. The money drawn from us by the three-penny tax on tea, and the stamp act, was not worth fighting about, except as it involved principle.

But had we yielded the principle that England might tax us at pleasure, who can tell what taxes she might have laid?—what burdens imposed? She might have ground us to the dust, and made us hewers of wood and drawers of water, to her wants, or pride or extravagance.

In the last war for Sailors' Rights, the case was much the same. The number of sailors impressed was not so great, nor their condition on board the British fleet so deplorable, (they fared as the British sailors did) as to make a resort to war indispensable, leaving out of view the rights involved. But had we given up the right of search and impressment, who can tell to what extent it might have gone? Who can tell how many thousands might have been torn from house and home and all that was dear, and made to spend their lives in fighting the battles of England?

We might refer to the political questions now agitated with so much earnestness between the National and State Governments, and their adherents. Rights are the bone of contention. And they are contended for with a zeal which proves that their worth is understood. It is seen, and felt, and avowed, that with our rights is connected every thing that is dear; that if they be lost, all is lost; if they be saved, all is safe.

That our rights are more important than anything else of which we can be deprived—that we may receive a deeper injury in our rights, than in any other way, (and of course may do a greater injury to another in his rights) is on the whole, well understood by the mass of the people. They have been pretty well schooled on this matter.

Now to see a professor of religion who is thus alive to the worth of rights; thus alive to the deep and irreparable injury which he may receive from that quarter; and who professes obedience to the command of his Lord, to "Love his neighbour as himself"—"To do in all things as he would be done by,"—to see him, in applying this rule to the case of slavery, pass over the whole matter of rights, the very part where he is most alive in his own case—the very part where the deepest wound may be given—the greatest injustice committed—and busy himself about the quantity of bread, and meat, and clothing, which will satisfy the rule—what shall we say of it! "What man seeing this, and having human feelings, does not blush, and hang his head to think himself a man."

What were the rights we were like to lose at the commencement of the revolutionary war? and to prevent which we entered into that fearful strife? The right of not being taxed but with our own consent. And what were the rights contended for in the last war? The rights of not being subject to search and impressment. These rights were, in the view of the people at large, worth contending for unto blood. The great bulk of professing Christians thought so too, and gave ample proof that they approved of the war, as right and necessary, by contributing their part to support it; and many of them by treading the tented field and mingling in the strife of battle.

Now, what are these rights compared with the rights of which the slave is deprived? They are mere nothing! and how can the Christian slave-holder say, he obeys Christ, "he does as he would be done by?"

But it will, perhaps, be said, that slaves don't know their rights; they have never possessed them and can't estimate their loss! Now passing the generosity and justice of withholding from a fellow creature his rights, because he is ignorant of them, or unable to assert them, I would like to know how it is reconciled with the morality of the gospel? what part of the teaching of Christ or his apostles, gives the shadow of authority for a course of conduct of this kind? How can it be reconciled with the rule of "doing as we would be done by?"

Apply the principle to the case of property. An orphan has right to property; but owing to some untoward circumstance in which he has been placed in infancy, and kept ever afterwards, he knows but little, if anything of his rights. The whole matter is so situated, that while his right is good, his neighbor can keep him from the possession of it, and, to a great degree, ignorant of his right to it, and destitute of the information needful to make the best use of it, where he in any way to get it in possession.

What now would we say of the honesty of that neighbor, who would take advantage in such a case? What would we say of his excuse, "he does not know the property is his;" "he does not know his rights;" "he can make no estimate of his loss." And how much would he mend the matter in the eyes of every honest man were he to say the person whose property I hold, not only does not know that it is his, or at least I can hold it in spite of him; but he is too ignorant to make a good use of it, if he had it; when it was notorious that he had kept him in ignorance, as a means of keeping him from his rights? And were this defrauder and oppressor to plead the example of others who acted in the same way; where he to plead that every man with a white face in his neighborhood, treated every one with a yellow or a black face, as he did the orphan boy, how much would he help his cause? Were he to profess the religion of the Lord Jesus, and take his seat at the sacramental table, while he still held on to the wages of unrighteousness, what would we say of his profession? what would we say of his religion? Suppose he were heard to say, and with great self-complacency, "I am good to the orphan boy; I have, it is true, stripped him of his all, but I am not cruel to him. I give him bread and meat when he passes, and at times make him presents of my old clothes."

How would public indignation brand such conduct. How would the report of it spread from Dan to Beersheba; and how would his name, blotted with disgrace, be handed down to posterity.

Now what is the loss of property compared with the loss of liberty? what is poverty compared with slavery? and on what page of Scripture is the rule of justice, of doing as we would be done by, suspended, when we meet with a man with a black face.

RESISTANCE TO OPPRESSION.

BY J. QUINCY, JR.

To complain of the enormities of power, to expostulate with overgrown oppressors, hath in all ages been denominated sedition and faction; and to turn upon tyrants, treason and rebellion. But tyrants are rebels against the first laws of heaven and society; to oppose their ravages is an instinct of nature—the inspiration of God in the heart of man. In the noble resistance which mankind make to exorbitant ambition and power, they always feel that divine afflatus which, paramount to every thing human, causes them to consider the Lord of Hosts as their leader, and his angels as fellow-soldiers. Trumpets are to them joyful sounds, and the ensigns of war the banners of God. Their wounds are bound up in the oil of a good cause; sudden death is to them present martyrdom, and funeral obsequies resurrections to eternal honor and glory,—their widows and babes being received into the arms of a compassionate God, and their names enrolled among David's worthies:—greatest losses are to them greatest gains; for they leave the troubles of their warfare to lie down on beds of eternal rest and felicity.

LIST OF ANTI-SLAVERY EVENTS.

The following is a list of anti-Slavery "events" which have occurred during the first four years of the rebellion:

1. Emancipation in Western Virginia.

2. Emancipation in Missouri.

3. Emancipation in the District of Columbia.

4. Emancipation in Maryland.

5. Slavery abolished and forever prohibited in all the Territories.

6. Kansas admitted as a free State.

7. Provisions made to admit Colorado, Nebraska and Nevada as free States.

8. Organization of Idaho, Montano, Decotah and Arizona as free Territories.

9. Recognition of the independence of Hayti and Liberia.

10. Three millions of slaves declared free by Proclamation of the President, Jan. 1, 1863.

11. All Fugitive Slave Laws repealed.

12. Inter-slave trade abolished.

13. Negroes admitted to equal rights in United States courts, as parties to suits and as witnesses.

14. Equality of the negro recognized in the public conveyances of the District of Columbia.

15. All rebel States prohibited from returning to the Union with slavery.

16. Free labor established on numerous plantations in South Carolina, Louisiana, Mississippi, Tennessee and Arkansas.

17. Schools for the education of freed slaves in South Carolinia, Tennessee, Lousiana, and in Eastern Virginia—where, till within three years, to educate the negro was punishable with death.

18. The wives and children of all slaves employed

as freemen in military and other service of the United States made free.

19. All negroes, bond and free, enrolled as part of the military force of the nation.

20. The loyal people of Arkansas, Tennessee, Louisiana and Florida seeking a return to the Union on the basis of freedom to all, and of the abolition and prohibition of slavery.

21. The abolition and prohibition of slavery by an amendment of the Constitution passed in the Senate by a two-thirds majority, and by nearly the same in the House. Lost by lack of three or four votes.

22. The nation through its representatives in Baltimore, June 8, made the abolition and prohibition of slavery the basis of its governmental administration for the future.

23. The Federal government forbidden to employ any man as a *slave* in any capacity.

24. One hnndred and fifty thousand negroes, mostly freed slaves, in the pay and uniform of the Government as soldiers.

Number of slaves freed in Maryland, 87,188; in Delaware, 592; District of Columbia, 3,185; Virginia, 163,629; Tennessee, 183,912; Louisiana, 201,150; South Carolina, 67,066; North Carolina, 55,176; Georgia, 154,066; Mississippi, 145,540, and Alabama, 145,023.

TABLE LIST OF MORTALITY.

Mortality lessens in the world as civilization and improvement advances. In England,

In 1700,	the deaths were as		1 in 25.
1780,	do.	do.	1 in 40
1790,	do.	do.	1 in 45.
1800,	do.	do.	1 in 47.
1810,	do.	do.	1 in 50.

In London, from 1700 to 1750, deaths were as 3 to 2; from 1750 to 1800, as 5 to 4; since 1800, as 12 to 15.

In Sweden, from 1755 to 1775, deaths were 1 in 35; from 1775 to 1795, as 1 in 37.

Of 100 new born infants in 1780, there died in two years, 50; at present, 38.

In 1780, died before ten years old....	55
At present........................	47
Lived in 1780, to 50 years..........	21
Live now to 50....................	32
Lived in 1780, to 60................	15
Live now to 60....................	24

The Language of Nature,

COMPARED WITH

DIVINE REVELATION.

Would you study Nature to find out God?
'Tis spirit only can read the record.

THE LANGUAGE OF NATURE.

I.

The heavens declare the glory of God,
In unison with his blessed word;
In the firmament his power is seen
Proclaiming the great Creator's reign;
Day unto day uttereth speech to the soul—
Night unto night showeth knowledge as of old.

II.

Think ye silence has no sound, and that hence
All is mute over Nature's wide expanse?
So with the sight, for 'tis equally true
That much lies hid from the natural view.
The eyes of the soul see in spirit-light,
And comprehend not the natural night.
As sense agrees to sense, so soul with soul;

One's mortal—the other's a living whole.
Would you study Nature to find out God?
'Tis spirit only can read the record.
Seek, then, with harmony of soul the light.
And unseen worlds will open to your sight.

III.

Close, then, the ear—shut out the grosser sound,
  And hear in every thing a living voice;
If sense disturb not this silence profound,
  The soul with vocal nature will rejoice.
Although Nature has charms for ears and eyes,
  Let not the outward sense the mind control;
But rather seek that which underlies
  The surface. Let soul commune with soul.

IV.

Inanimate nature is but a name,
  For organized life is every where,
While the eye sees it only on the wing,
  Soul penetrates the rôck and finds it there.
Here are the workings of infinite mind;
  And with what amazing mystery fraught!

Here matchless wisdom and power combined
  Unfold a page for venerated thought.

V.

Bow, then, O my soul! in grateful prayer
Before thy God, who is present here;
Think not he dwells only in the skies;
Behold, he is *here*, all Nature cries.
Up, down, have a mere relative sense,
And are lost in Nature's vast expanse.
Then say not of God, he's here or there,
For the spirit sees him every where.
Come, then, O thou child of immortal birth!
Together we'll visit old mother earth.

VI.

Venerable parent! mother of all!
  As we tread thy vast chambers, grant us light;
'Tis falsely said that darkness, like a pall,
  Locks up thy courts in one eternal night;
For a record is here, faithful and true,
  Written in characters that cannot lie;

Unfading as the rock on which we view
The footprints of ages as they pass by.

VII.

And living creatures, all sportive and free,
  Have their existence in thy great warm heart;
Each one fulfilling its own destiny,
  And each acting out its allotted part.
'Tis thus thy maternal bosom doth swell
  With life infinite in degree and form,
'Til each particle of earth, and each cell,
Is the happy home of insect or worm.

VIII.

And here life and death together blend,
And in death life finds a constant friend;
For death, we do see, is but a name,
And is swallowed up of life again.
I gaze upon the velvet lawn
And think, as life begins to dawn,
(Seeing death changed to living green,
The type of never-ending Spring,)

That then I fain would lay me down
To repose in death's friendly arm.

IX.

O matchless wisdom and love profound!
Lo! every where ye do abound,
Dispersing the gloom of darkness and night,
And filling the soul with refreshing light;
E'en here in Nature's book we read
How death but sows a living seed.

X.

If a man die shall he live again?
E'en Nature will make the question plain;
Things from one state to another live on,
And death assumes life in some other form.
Thus nothing is lost in nature, we see,
And here the soul reads its own destiny;
For man is a nobler creation still,
And is destined a higher sphere to fill.

XI.

O thou uncreated great first cause!
Man every where may read thy laws

In the flowery plain and meadow green,
Infinite power is plainly seen;
The roaring torrent and babbling brook,
The lofty pine and giant oak,
Do each in Nature's book record
The glorious truth — there is a God.

XII.

The feathered songster, warbling there,
In ev'ry note he does declare
(As it vibrates sweetly on the air)
A Creator kind and good;
And as he sings from tree to tree,
O thoughtless man! he speaks to thee,
Ever saying, "Come learn of me;
Be grateful for your daily food."

XIII.

There is a God; the lightning flies,
Bearing the truth along the skies;
The rolling thunders too plainly speak
Of a Creator mighty and great;

The truth is declared again and again
By the rising vapor and falling rain.

XIV.

But hark! another witness still!
  What music soft and sweet!
'Tis the sound of the little rill;
  How sweetly it doth speak.
'Tis eventide—I'll sit me down,
  And while Nature's hushed in sleep,
I'll listen to your merry sound,
  And with thee thy vigils keep.

XV.

Come tell me, O thou silvan stream!
  As so softly you pass along.
Where going?—whither hast thou been?
  I fain would listen to your song.
Thou speak'st to me of olden time,
  And still thou art flowing:
Come, tell me of that foreign clime
  Whither thou art going.

XVI.

And speak to me of mighty powers,
  Of life in many forms;
And speak to me of sunny bowers,
  Of dark and pelting storms.
Yes, speak to me of fleecy gold,
  Scenes radiant in the sky,
Where magic beauty you unfold
  To the admiring eye.
But onward, onward, you cannot stay;
  We will meet, perchance, some other day;
In the gentle rain or early dew,
  I'll seek again, sweet friend, for you.

XVII.

But nature, every where the same,
Keeps up the inexhaustible theme;
If from one subject you turn away,
Another will meet you on your way;
Thus you read her glorious record,
That leads from Nature to Nature's God.

XVIII.

So the mind, ever anxious to soar,
Never content, ever grasping more,
Looks into space, when every where
Unseen wonders do ever appear.
The air, of which man ever hath need,
In the laws of nature 'tis decreed,
That go where he will, 'twill seek him there,
Whether he give thanks or e'en forbear;
Pressed gently by that, he can't feel or see,
And moving with intense velocity,
Yet pillowed all round with elastic air,
He passes on insensible of fear.

XIX.

Of life, it is the all-pervading source,
So soft, and yet what an amazing force!
The atmospheric pressure that surrounds
The body is thirty-two thousand pounds,
And yet, strange to say, 'tis not felt by man,
For a corresponding pressure within

(And that which surrounds each and every part)
Equilibriates the force and protects the heart.

XX.

Nature's great laboratory here
Receives a purified atmosphere;
No decomposed matter can remain,
But all is restored to life again.
Faithful minister! how much we learn,
As thy mysterious work goes on!

XXI.

And then from death to life you turn,
Seeking it in its early morn,
The needful source of life supplying,
The same you gathered from the dying;
How strange! what mind should not here pause
To contrast natural with moral laws!

XXII.

'Tis Nature's philosophy we see,
(And shall not theology agree?)
That *death* is *a mean*, and not an *end*,
As some very pious souls pretend.

It corruption puts on life again
Must not incorruption remain ?
Thus Nature teaches a better way,
Than some great minds of the present day.
But I turn, dame Nature, again to you;
Your teachings are ever faithful and true.

XXIII.

And God made a wind to pass over the earth,
In which he commanded the air to go forth,
For wind is air in motion, and here
His wisdom and goodness both appear;
For if the air did quiet remain,
Inland would perish for want of rain,
But the clouds are driven to and fro,
Scattering blessings where'er they go.

XXIV.

And then, as the mighty winds prevail,
Filling the anxious mariner's sail,
A highway's marked out upon the seas,
Where a messenger, by ev'ry breeze,

Bears love and fraternal friendship abroad,
Binding the nations with its golden cord.

XXV.

Then on, ye white-winged messengers of hope!
On your mission of truth and love, nor stop
'Til heathen lands shall be fruitful and grow
The seed that God sends his servants to sow;
'Til her waste places blossom as the rose,
And there be none to hinder or oppose.

XXVI.

Rejoice, then, O ye servants of God!
As you bear abroad his blessed word;
Rejoice, O ye ends of the earth!
Rejoice in God's eternal truth!
Jesus has triumphed—made an end of sin—
And now he invites you to glory with him.

XXVII.

But the winds not only on the seas
Do God's bidding, but among the trees;
These are compelled due homage to pay,
In bowing their heads so gracefully.

Reader, do you pray? If not, then see
And learn a lesson, e'en from the tree.

XXVIII.

But they also sing, and would you hear?
Go to the forest, and there in prayer
Seek, in harmony of spirit,
The inspiration to inherit.
The soul once tuned to these melodies,
Would fondly linger among the trees.

XXIX.

If your thoughts with profit you'd employ,
Just see with what animated joy
Each tiny leaf, like a living thing,
Moves as if conscious of life within.
'Tis even so, for here, in the sun,
Countless creatures live in sportive fun;
Although mysterious it doth appear,
Each leaf's a world in its own little sphere.
Omnipotent power! for here we see
Worlds multiplied as the sands of the sea.

XXX.

And God said, "Let there be light;"
  And as man alone may disobey;
Chaotic darkness takes its flight
  Before the rising God of day.
Well might the morning stars sing for joy,
Their anthems in rapture repeat,
As the new creation shouts the cry,
"Welcome twin sisters—"*Light and Heat!*"

XXXI.

Amazing wonder! majestic sight!
Thy life-giving heat and golden light
Fill with joy the ecstatic soul,
As revolving worlds around thee roll!
How strange, as the hoary ages roll on,
That man should cease to wonder at the sun.

XXXII.

Light and heat penetrate all bodies,
And thus become most pleasing studies;
E'en a piece of crude and silent steel
Will the most important truths reveal.

Here lies an element cold and dark,
But strike the flint, it will give a spark,
Though for ages silent and unseen
Will kindle a vast devouring flame,
Or in a mild and radiant glow,
A genial heat on all bestow.

XXXIII.

In wonder I gaze as I see thee burn;
  Although my senses you would lock in sleep,
From your carbon ashes how much I learn!
  And 'tis thus, I'll suppose, I hear thee speak:

XXXIV.

"Despise me not as here I lay,
  Although unseemly to the sight;
On wings transparent I'll fly away,
  And, after resting on alpine height,
You'll meet me in some tiny flower,
Where light and heat combine their power."

XXXV.

Come tell me then, O thou kingly rose!
As your magic blushes you disclose,

Decomposing the rays of solar light,
Sending the red only to our sight,
Why is your loveliness so complete?
Do you absorb and radiate heat?
Ah! yes; and then you are wrapt within
The warm ærial mantle of Spring.

XXXVI.

King of flowers, 'tis in you I find
A gratitude far excelling mine;
The gaseous vapours you absorb
In common with ev'ry plant and herb;
After which you do again restore
To man a pure, healthy atmosphere.

XXXVII.

The carbon and hydrogen man don't need,
And upon these you are content to feed;
As a thanksgiving for the early dew,
A sweet odor on all you do bestow;
Then in your death what a lesson you teach!
How eloquently of beauty you preach!

XXXVIII.

Pause, then, vain beauty, as you pass by,
See those fading leaflets as there they lie;
Thy charms will so perish—ah! how soon
Must they return to the waiting tomb!

XXXIX.

'Tis thus Nature speaks through the fading rose,
And should it not cause us to cherish
Thoughts of that beauty which ever more glows,
And not of that which thus must perish?

XL.

Yes, when we look into this starry space, this eternity of vastness, how the soul trembles and pants for its ærial flight! Like the reined charger, it is restless and eager for the race, and oh! what a race! what an eternal round of infinite progression!

But we will invite the reader's attention to a further contemplation (in prose) of the great centre of this universe of worlds that infinite power and wisdom has hung in space. And as we can draw very suitable comparisons between this and the Savior of mankind, (he being the centre of the moral universe,) our remarks will be accompanied with such reflections as may suggest themselves, first observing that as the entire planetary system is dependent on the sun for light and heart, (which is the life and soul of nature,) so all souls are dependent on Christ, the light of the moral universe, that lighteth every man that cometh into the world. It is from this source we receive that flame of love which burns upon the altar of the heart, and that purifies and inspires the soul. And how beautifully parallel are the laws of attraction! As none of the members of the natural system can pass the bounds of these laws, it is fair to conclude from Nature's stand-point, that not one member of the human family, however outward appearances might seem to justify an opposite belief, will ever pass entirely beyond that attraction and saving power which God has invested in his son, and which constitutes him the Savior of all men. "When I am lifted up," says the Savior, "I will draw all men unto me."

Thus Nature is the preface of God's great book;
Revelation completes the glorious work.
Nature is the twilight, revelation the sun;
God's the author of both, and their teachings are one.

Mysterious orb! thou god of light, and world of worlds, whose infinite rays, marshaled in thine own glory, fills all space and wraps in splendor a dependent universe! Who can behold thy spangled crest, those converging rays and golden beams, without awe and delight? With what majestic grandeur this world of flaming fire takes leave of his earthly child! See with what apparent tenderness he draws in those life-giving rays, still lingering upon the velvet lawn, loth, as it were, to undo affection's embrace! and as each cloud parts with its lining of crimson; as those golden threads are woven into robes of transcendent loveliness, with what majestic splendor he gathers them about him, and gracefully drops behind the western hills. And now as the evening shades close o'er this scene of indescribable beauty, a voice whispers, "'Tis the hour of prayer!" Twilight, with her sable veil, has covered the face of Nature, and the robin, whose last note still trembles upon the passing breeze, has gone to his nest. The cattle of a thousand hills, whose tinkling bells still vibrate upon the air, have laid them down in quiet repose. All Nature is hushed in silence—a silence that speaks with inspired eloquence to the soul, saying, "How sacred is this hour!" Arise, then, O my soul! and to Nature's consecrated temple thy offering bring! Here bow thee and worship the living God.

Here all things are pure and undefiled
Save thyself, O thou immortal child
  Of God; but thou,
With wisdom and intelligence blest,
As a slave to sin, that knows no rest,
  Do'st deign to bow?
But the way of the transgressor's hard,
And ev'ry act has its own reward.
No peace to the wicked, yet there's given
Saving grace to all, and rest in heaven.

But see, as the ev'ning shades prevail,
The moon takes up the wondrous tale.
How gracefully her silv'ry light
Inaugurates the reign of night!

How majestically she glides along, as ever and anon an additional star makes its appearance, until the whole canopy of heaven is resplendent with the glory of revolving worlds. Grand and imposing scene! And is this, as some would say, the work of chance: worlds thrown into space, suspended in air, and ever revolving with an exactness measured only by the minutest division of time? Never! 'Tis the fool who says in his heart, "There is no God."

O thou omnipotent power who do'st sprinkle with worlds this eternity of space! thou God of love and universal Father, grant that while the mind contemplates this vast and expansive dome of light, that the soul, on the wings of faith, may soar beyond to the still greater glory of the spirit world, the heavenly spheres, where angelic intelligences ever rejoice in the presence of God.

Dear reader, this is the goal of thy soul's aspirations. And would you be one of this happy and glorified throng? Remember that nothing unclean or defiled can enter the kingdom of heaven. 'Tis the Father's good will to gather all his children to this their heavenly home, through the power of omnipresent and infinite love; yea, e'en though by scourging it purge thy soul of all its dross, and bring thee once more as a little child to commence thy career of eternal glory.

We have seen that God is present in all his works. Now, it is this divine presence (felt and realized) that constitutes the soul's heaven, whether in this or any other state; and the degrees of heaven are just in proportion to the spiritual development. In the present state, the law of the mind being frequently brought into subjection to the law of the flesh, it naturally follows that the energies of the soul become weakened, and God's presence less felt and enjoyed. From this it will be seen that just as the soul is kept pure and undefiled by sin, will its enjoyment increase, itself rise higher in the atmosphere of spirit-life, and approximate nearer to the divine essence.

Thus sin separates the soul from God, and causes man to wander an alien. We do not intend entering upon an examination of the nature of sin, nor what part man has to perform in its removal; whether he is to be re-created, endowed with new faculties, or whether those he possesses are to be appealed to and quickened. Neither do we intend discussing the Atonement, whether man's guilt be expiated by an infliction of the punishment and sufferings due his own sins upon an innocent person, or whether the sufferings of the Savior were not the natural result of his mission, and had no further merit than just in proportion as they formed the attracting power to bring man back to his God. Suffice it to say, that salvation consists in being delivered from the power and thraldom of sin; hence Christ's mission to the children of men. His name shall be called Jesus, for he shall save his people from their sins. "Behold the Lamb of God that taketh away the sin of the world," &c., &c. There are many pious souls who do not seem to believe this Scripture; nevertheless, God is in Christ reconciling the world unto himself. Now suppose the great work of reconciliation be not completed in man's present state, will he therefore fail to accomplish that which he purposed in himself before the world began? or, rather, will not the reign of grace be extended to the spirit-world, (and no other view can harmonize the Scriptures with themselves and these with the attributes of God,) and man there continue his career of eternal progression from the highest point of moral improvement attained here? with, however, this very important advantage: Instead of a body ever at variance with the spirit, in consequence of its antagonistic propensities and inclination to moral death, ("for the flesh lusteth to sin, and sin, when it is finished, brings forth death"); instead, I say, of being encumbered with this body of death, he will enjoy a complete deliverance from it, for in the resurrection this corruption will put on incorruption, the natural be changed to the spiritual, and the soul thus disencumbered will stretch forth her wings, and with glorified body,

> Rise higher and higher,
> With increasing desire.

Thus the enjoyments of heaven will ever increase with the soul's increasing capacity. From the above we are led to believe that the old notion of heaven, as a place with certain bounds and limitations, over which a very large portion of God's children can never pass, is a delusion of the dark ages; and with all deference to those who hold this belief, we are constrained to say, that truth is progressive, and that those who stand still must expect to be left behind. The kingdom of heaven is a state and condition of the mind, and is therefore within us; and this truth will be realized just in proportion as we pass from under the reign of darkness, error and sin, into the broad, open light of the gospel of God's dear Son. The Scriptures surely nowhere indicate that the reign of grace will be suspended while one unreconciled soul remains. In what other sense can Jesus be the Savior of *all* men? He came to seek that which is lost, and we are assured that he will not give up the kingdom to the Father until the last enemy be put under his feet, and he shall see of the travail of his soul and be satisfied. This, dear reader, is the great and good Shepherd that careth for the sheep. Think you if every soul but *one* were saved, he would desert *that soul?* In the parable of the lost sheep we have an answer to this question, and a true representation of the nature and character of the blessed Savior's mission. Here we see the world's Redeemer going out in pursuit of the lost one, nor does he cease seeking until he finds it, bearing it in his own loving bosom to the fold. This is the great centre and sun of the moral universe. His attractions may not be felt for the time being — an eclipse may have hid him from view — but he shines nevertheless; yea, and will continue to shine until all are brought to feel the power of his divine rays, and until the waters of iniquity that have deluged the soul be broken up, and pass off in tears of joy and repentance.

Then crucify the body with all its fleshly lusts, and the soul, thus unfettered, will naturally rise and seek its affinity with the Father of all Spirits. The resurrection will produce no miraculous change in man's nature, for the same faculties and the same identity will exist. Man is not a passive being; and as glory ever points upward, he will have to ascend to it, instead of its descending upon him. God works by means, and these are always abundant; but man, alas! is ever prone to disregard them, in consequence of which he wanders a prodigal away from his God, and feeds upon the husks of sin in a foreign land. Now, the resurrection is one of the great means of restoration. Here the soul is delivered from its prison house, and the many fleshly hindrances having been left behind in the grave, it is once more free to exercise its normal powers.

But it seeks its freedom here ;
Why, then, wait for another sphere ?
With *effort* you will have to rise,
Whether on earth or in the skies.

God, both in Nature and in grace,
In every thing in every place,
Reveals a loving, smiling face,
And ever seeks to bless.
When the earth puts forth her increase,
  'Tis for thee.
When birds sing sweetly from place to place,
  'Tis for thee;
When flowers bloom in early Spring,
  'Tis for thee;
When the clouds drop refreshing rain,
  'Tis for thee;
God provides abundance of air
  For thee;
Bright waters sparkle ev'ry where
  For thee;
This universe he hung in space
  For thee;
In the blessed Savior's death,
Oh! what amazing love and grace
  For thee!

Then may I ever grateful be
To thee, O Father! for I see
In Nature thou dost care for me,
And my daily wants supply.
Thy blessings scattered all around,
In touch, in taste, in sight, in sound,
Thy love and grace to all abound,
And all may feel thee nigh.
Grant, O Father! this boon to man,
That all may rightly understand
Thy all-wise and loving plan,
To reconcile all to thee.
For, as the rain's impartial fall,
So faith, repentance, is for all.
The rich, the poor, the great, the small,
Shall all thy glory see.

Dear reader, what a glorious hope is this! May it purify our hearts, and make us fit companions for that innumerable throng who have entered within the vale

Where they cast their bright and starry crowns
  At the Redeemer's feet;
High in the heavens the echo sounds,
  As his praises they repeat:
Crying, holy, holy, is the lamb,
Worthy art thou to reign,
As in robes of light they march around
The Savior's shining throne.
This glorious, rapturous scene,
  We worms of earth may share,
For soon (oh! joy!) this world of sin
  In death will disappear.
The battle is o'er, the victory's won,
The conquering Savior proclaims 'tis done!
'Tis finished, O Father! and sealed with the cross;
All souls were mine—"all are returned without loss."

The reader will pardon this digression, as our subject would naturally lead to such thoughts and reflections. We have endeavored to show that God wills that all men shall be saved and brought to a knowledge of the truth. So *we read* in Nature and in revelation; but just as sure as the child that puts its finger in the fire is burned, so sure will every transgression or act of disobedience (whether to natural or revealed laws) meet with a just recompense of reward.

> There is a world all desolate and dark;
> 'Tis neither up, nor down, *but in the heart.*
> "Woe!" is the password to this dismal hell,
> And its tortures all guilty souls must feel.

Men cannot transgress the laws of God with impunity; but we believe all punishments to be *disciplinary* and *reformatory*, inflicted for an all-wise purpose, and that this purpose will not fail. As for the origin of evil, (although it has greatly perplexed the most able minds,) we do not think it so dark a subject. "Man was created subject to vanity, not willingly, but by reason of him who subjected the same in hope." Here is light, and none could fail to see it, did not a false theology make evil an *end* instead of a *means.* God, the great First Cause, the Creator, the Redeemer, *our Father,* reigns and rules.

We are firm and happy in the belief that *all men* (in the end) will be the better for having passed through this lower school of experience, and that the sufferings and afflictions of this present life "will work for us a far more exceeding and eternal weight of glory."

GOD IN EVERY THING.

[From the Millennial Harbinger.)

The intellect of man has undergone a great revolution since the development of the inductive mode of reasoning. For many centuries the dialectics of Aristotle governed the whole mental world, and kept in logical fetters the intellect of the human race; but we have happily been delivered from this thraldom, and the progress of knowledge in a very few years has been truly astonishing.

The ancients loved to speculate upon the abstract essences of spirit and matter, and the keen subtlety of their intellect peculiarly fitted them for this kind of investigation; but the moderns, wholly unlike them, critically analyze all things they are called on to believe, or upon which they are to act.

In this change we have lost that glowing enthusiasm — that high-wrought ideality which distinguished those of the olden time, and perhaps, likewise, we have lost too much of that deep veneration which characterized their minds when looking upon the grand or awful display of the phenomena of nature. This effect, however, might be anticipated from the course of popular education which tends to give a knowledge of the universe wholly abstracted from the great source of all things, and this great error has undermined that high religious feeling, and induced an inflated scepticism which presumes to explain every effect in nature by some physical cause, not perceiving that every created cause is but an effect, and that God is the great *first cause* of all things.

The grand central thought in all correct education is to lead the youthful mind to see God in every thing. While it gives a correct knowledge of all causes and effects known to man, it never permits Jehovah to be lost sight of, or a hard and unfeeling analysis to take the place of that profound veneration which listens to the solemn reverberations of the thunder through the deep vault of heaven, as the best earthly emblem of the voice of the Almighty. While it displays the laws which govern the life of the animalcule which floats in the sunbeam, and the giant mammoth of the ages gone by, it stops not at the law, but elevates the mind to that Being who could display his power in a thing so minute as perfectly as in one so grand. While it explains the principles which govern the life of the vegetable world, it comments upon the inimitable beauty of the tiny flower and the commanding majesty of the lofty cedar as but another evidence of the kindness of our heavenly Father in thus giving us both the beautiful and useful to add to our happiness in time. In short, true education never stops short of the throne of God; for the grand intention of all correct instruction is to make us love him more ardently and adore him more profoundly.

The whole universe is full of benevolent design. We cannot take a single step without perceiving fresh displays of the work of an almighty hand. Around, above and beneath us, we see God in every thing. Let us look for a short time at the constitution of our atmosphere, as a beautiful illustration of the love and wisdom of God in providing for the happiness of man.

The air we breathe is one of the most abundant things of which chemistry treats. Animals and plants, from the lowest to the highest grade, depend upon it for life. The first act of the infant is to inhale the air, and the last mortal struggle of the dying man is an effort to catch its inspiring breath. This fluid surrounding the earth to the distance of about forty-five miles, and so nicely adapted to be the home of every thing that breathes, has been the object of profound study to the learned in all ages, and was long considered as an element; but modern analysis has proved it to be a compound, made up of two gasses—oxygen and nitrogen—so perfectly balanced for the support of life, that to take from or add to either principle, would totally defeat the end contemplated. This is the only fluid with which we are acquainted that would support life. Oxygen is the vivifying principle: it gives beauty to the cheek and vigor to the frame; and, combined with carbon, is the cause of animal heat. Nitrogen is a negative principle, which acts, so far as we can judge, merely to dilute the oxygen. No other gas, except nitrogen could be mixed with oxygen so as to answer the end of our atmosphere. Hydrogen may be temporarily combined with it, and animals and plants might live in it for a short time, but derangement of all the vital functions would be the effect of a continuous respiration of it. Animals kept in it for any length of time become dull and stupid as if exposed to narcotic influence. If this had been the constitution of our atmosphere, instead of the active life now every where manifested, a universal gloom and lethargy would seize upon every living thing; thus making this fair creation a place of silence and of death.

But another effect, even more disastrous than this, would be the consequence of such an atmospheric constitution. Oxygen and hydrogen form a most explc sive mixture; combined in certain proportions. a sin gle spark of fire would make it flash like gunpowder; and thus the earth would be destroyed by a universal conflagration; so that we would be exposed at any moment to the most horrible of all disasters—a raging fire, which nothing could quench. If there was any other compound which would answer the end of our atmosphere, the sceptic might appear to have some ground for triumph; but the absence of all such is an incontestible proof that the Being who made the frame of man designed and prepared the atmosphere for the support of his animal life.

But the evidence of design does not end in the choice of principles. It extends to the proportions in which they are invariably found mixed. If oxygen prevailed in the atmosphere to a greater extent than at present, every living thing would soon be exhausted by the intensity of its action, as the fire is soonest extinguished which burns with the greatest fierceness, and thus the earth would become as silent as the tomb from the unwise preponderance of a principle which, in its present diluted state, gives life and energy to all animated nature.

Again, if nitrogen were mixed in greater volume than at present, a hebitude would steal over every faculty of mind and body. The blood, wanting its needful stimulus, would cease its active flow, and in a purple current would creep through the lifeless veins. The intellect, sympathizing with the paralyzed frame, would cease its action,—reason would refuse her office—imagination would fold her wings, and even the religious feeling would cease to fill the heart with its glad and elevated inspiration. Thus we see that if we either alter the constituents or change the proportions of the atmosphere, we destroy the work of the All-Wise, who has adapted every thing to the wants of his creatures.

But every thing that breathes and burns makes war upon this balance so exquisite and uniform. The countless fires upon the face of the earth are supported altogether by oxygen. The myriads of animals which breathe the breath of life, absorb the oxygen and give back to the air carbonic acid gas, a poisonous compound, which, when inspired, is destructive to human life. How, then, is the equilibrium between the constituents of the atmosphere maintained, which is so constantly invaded by such potent enemies? By what wise adjustment is harmony made to triumph over the principles of discord?

If the gasses were governed by that law which keeps bodies of the greatest specific gravity nearest the earth, then carbonic acid gas, which is more than twice the weight of the atmosphere, would settle all over the surface of the earth, and thus this beautiful creation, like the grotto at Naples, would be filled with a vapor destructive of life.

But this casualty was foreseen by the Omniscient Eye, and a bountiful provision made for it. The particles of each gas are so constructed that they press only in kindred particles, and offer but a slight resistance to the free passage of any other gas. Thus the two gasses of which the atmosphere is composed readily permeate each other's interstices, and the carbonic acid, though much heavier than the air, rises into it without difficulty, for the particles of air resting upon each other, are to the acid as if a vacuum existed above it; and in this manner the surface of the earth is relieved from what would be its destruction.

But the purity of the atmosphere would still be invaded by the presence of too great a quantity of this poisonous gas, and the wisdom of the Maker is strikingly displayed in the provision by which it is reduced to a healthful ratio.

Vegetables find in carbonic acid their most acceptable food, and absorb it with avidity. But this absorption might, in time, rob the atmosphere of too much of its oxygen. This would be the case if the plant had not the power to separate the constituents of the acid, to mingle the carbon with its own tissues, and throw off the pure oxygen into the air again. It is in this way that every plant, shrub, flower and tree lends its influence to keep the vital breath around us free from a corrupt influence, which otherwise would poison the very source of life. Water also absorbs carbonic acid and returns pure oxygen to the air; thus aiding to prevent its too great accumulation.

We cannot too much admire the wisdom which provided for the maintenance of an equilibrium in an essential element of life, when accumulation of any one principle would be death. Thus the poisonous miasma floating in the atmosphere becomes so diluted with the life-giving principle that it becomes innoxious; and the air under the action of this law of gasses cannot become stagnant, for the particles easily glide over each other, and are constantly altering their position; consequently there can be no deleterious accumulation of any of the constituents of the atmosphere, nor of any foreign matter which circumstances might introduce into it.

Another beautiful provision to prevent the stagnation of the atmosphere deserves the admiration of the student. Heat rarifies it and causes it to ascend, and the colder and heavier body of air around rushes in to supply the place of the fluid which ascends. The effects of this law are truly admirable. The stratum of air which at one moment reclines upon the bosom of the earth, and which would in a short time become intensely heated, in the next moment ascends to the regions of frost, where it becomes heavier by cold, and then descends refreshed from its ærial flight to give its cool breath to the flowers upon the plains beneath. The sun, pouring his fiery rays directly upon the tropical regions, would render that part of the earth uninhabitable did not the ærial wave which to-day floats over the heated equator, ascend and bear its warmth to the polar ices; while the condensed atmosphere of the northern regions comes in to supply its place and gladden the tropics with its delicious coolness. Thus the great atmospheric ocean is constantly moving, and hence the phenomena of winds to which the atmosphere owes its vitality, purity and sweetness.

The air at rest is one of the worst conductors of heat; and if this apparently unimportant law were changed, and the air became a conductor, the earth could not be inhabited by man. The tongue placed upon a piece of steel on a morning when the thermometer is a few degrees from zero, instantly adheres to it by freezing, because the metal conducts the heat more rapidly from the tongue than it can be generated; and for a similar reason the fingers are quickly blistered by frozen mercury; it draws off their heat more quickly than they can generate it. Now suppose the air possessed the conducting power of the steel, our warmest clothing would be of no avail, houses could not shelter us, fire could not preserve us, In spite of every effort to preserve the vital warmth, it would soon become exhausted, and the human race, at a temperature above 32°, the freezing point of water, would become extinct. As it is, man braves the most intense cold of the polar winter, where the mercury freezes in the open air, and the only animal seen abroad after sunset is the arctic fox. The air in motion soon sinks the temperature of the human body, because each new wave abstracts a portion of heat. But it has been wisely ordered that in the coldest climates winds rarely blow in winter, and the animals of those frozen regions are clothed with furs and down, which, confining the air in their porous textures, become the worst of all conductors. Thus man, learning wisdom from nature, has appropriated to himself many of those admirable substances, and clothed in this panoply fearlessly commits himself to frozen oceans and icy poles.

It would take a long time to exhaust this subject, so full of beautiful adaptations, so rich in evidence of design. Who can doubt the existence and control of an all-wise Creator when contemplating laws so beautiful—adaptations so perfect. Methinks that a youth educated in this way to see the perfections of God in the constitution of the universe, might be exposed without fear to the influence of infidel principles; for the testimony is so ample and overwhelming, so perfectly familiar, and within his grasp, that if he has only been educated to see God in every thing, there is no adverse influence can touch him. The idea that so much wisdom is but the work of blind chance, is abhorrent to his mind; for he sees a benevolent Creator in earth, and sea, and sky, and he feels that "the heavens declare the glory of God, and the firmament showeth his handy work."

THE EARTH.

[From the Millennial Harbinger.)

It is evident that God would have us learn his character and glorious attributes, not only from revelation, but also from nature. He has implanted in us the desire to know the hidden causes of things—given us capacities whereby we may gratify that desire—and unrolled, in the broad volume of creation, inexhaustible pages of magnificence and wisdom, from which we can derive knowledge and instruction. The saints in all ages have delighted to hold converse with the still spirit that broods over this breathing world, and acknowledge, in the murmur of the rill, the roar of the torrent, the springing of the flower and the tough-rooted majesty of the oak, the gentle shower and the impetuous storm—in every accent loud or low, which in ten thousand voices awake the sublime evidences she ever and always utters of the goodness, wisdom and power

"*That plann'd, and built, and still upholds a world,*
So cloth'd with beauty for rebellious man."

Whether we look to the interior of our globe or confine our observation to its surface, we are filled with admiration at the vastness of the scale on which God has been, and is still operating for his fallen creatures. We have already adverted to those stupendous strides by which old chaos mounted, through successive formations, to what, in the poetry of our admiration, we are pleased to call the present beautiful earth, and seen in it all, how wonderful are his ways, with whom a thousand years are as one day and one day as a thousand years! But these are, in the main, the vailed wonders of the earthly tabernacle. They are the familiar altars of nature's High Priests only. They can only be approached with that full intimacy which makes them truly known by him who has caught incense from the altar of science, and can sprinkle his path with the sacrifice of many a toilsome hour of devotion. It is in this outer court that we may all enter and adore. The broad bosom of the earth is spread out in living colors before us, and we are invited by all its variety and vastness, to make its acquaintance. But its very attractions deter us. So manifold are its wonders—so intricate its mysteries, that we falter upon the threshold and have not courage to enter.

Much of our discouragement, however, arises from our own negligence to inquire, and much from the very artificial modes in which we have been taught to examine. All our systems of geography contemplate the earth more as a stage for political intrigue, a vast and complex amphitheatre, in which kings may tilt and subjects bleed—a mighty chess-board, on which the bloody game of war is played, for the regal prize of conquest, than as the footstool of Jehoval, the fallen object of his unwearied love, and the scene of that remedial grace, which works and energises in us and by us for the renovation and glory of man. It is to be lamented that in tracing out the artificial boundaries of kingdoms and numbering their subjects, we so often forget the broad outlines that God has given us, and that good which he designed by them, for his creatures. It is thus that the mind is turned away from the contemplation of the power of God to the glory of the king, and the wisdom and goodness of his gifts, to the prudence and forethought of an earth-born, like ourselves.

If we could fancy ourselves destitute of all this knowledge and gifted with the science to comprehend at a glance, the whole surface of our earth, we should find, that it is not flat as the ancient poets supposed, but a globe—almost a perfect sphere, with a surface diversified, not indeed by the lines of boundary between nations and the petty princes that lord it over its domains, but by those stronger and more enduring delineations of wisdom—seas, and continents and islands. In the arrangement, proportion and physical appearance of these, we should find much to marvel at and to study. We could not help being filled with astonishment at the vast preponderance of water over the general surface. Stand where we would, too, on the great bosom of the deep, we should find, that it was all a unit. Not many divisions, isolated and disconnected from each other, but all one great and unbroken circulation—feeling softly its way in the rivulet, or dashing, headlong and furious, in the torrent. Not a vibration wakes its pulse beneath us, that does not tremble to the remotest shores of its unmeasured reach;—but one and unsevered this great heart of the earth beats, the same on the coasts of Peru—against the icy barriers of the South—around the spicy isles of the East—amidst the regions of eternal sunshine, and the dreary solitudes of unmelting snows. God has measured it in the hollow of his hand, and there it waves, covering in its broad bosom a hundred and fifty millions of miles,—three-fourths of the entire surface of the globe, and sufficient in quantity to bury it all nearly eight thousand feet in water!

What an overwhelming spectacle is here! And at first, what an unmeaning waste of waters is thus rolling around us! But we look more closely, and how beautifully it is working, by God's appointment, for the comfort and happiness of man, tempering the vertical suns of the tropics and moderating the searching blasts of the poles—thus equalizing and controlling the otherwise disastrous changes of climate and making habitable and salubrious the abode of man. From its surface, too, are rising the restless vapors, which floats, by the breezes it creates, far to the inland fields, watering the thirsty earth, and keeping in abundant and exhaustless supplies the fountains of rivers and of lakes. That shower we see falling, and that river which

Labitur et labetur in omne volubilis ævum,

(Flows and shall flow through every age the same)—have both come from its bosom; and, after their long journey through the air, on the wings of the wind, are returning, by the simple laws of gravity, to their ocean home again. On its shores, countless throngs are settled, subsisting upon its ample stores of fish and salt, and looking for the white sail or the puffing steamer, which are borne on its bosom, from the distant zones of the earth, and laden with the luxuries they produce. Its great currents, too, pouring in their purified supplies from the poles, and keeping in perpetual motion the great mass of waters, preserve it ever fresh and uncorrupted, and show by what simple yet majestic compensations, God maintains the harmonies of his universe.

Turning our attention to that other portion of surface, we call the land, making about one-fourth only of the whole — we are filled, if possible, with more confusion than before. Standing over the eastern shore of the great island of New Holland, and turning our face towards the North — we shall see on our left, rising from the Cape of Good Hope, the great mountain chain of Africa, called "the Spine of the World;" before us, from the centre of Thibet, through Chinese Mongolia, towards Okotsk, and thence to the extreme eastern promontory of Asia, another vast chain of mountains stretching from southwest to north-east; and on our right—that vast and unbroken chain of the highest mountains on the globe, which ranges along the whole coast of America, from the Straits of Behring to Cape Horn, and closely borders, with its tremendous precipices, the shores of the great Pacific. We are thus in the midst of an immense circle, whose circumference, with only occasional breaks, is composed of lofty and inhospitable mountains, and within which is embraced the greater part of the waters of the earth. Between us and these, in the North, falling towards the ocean, is the great kingdom of China, called by themselves, possibly from its position, *Chium-hoa*, the *Middle Kingdom*. Beyond these mountains lies the great mass of the two continents into which the whole of the land surface is divided by the narrow Straits of Behring. If this were filled up, we should have but one continent and but one ocean. But what a variety is here! Detached and irregular mountains—high, but level table lands—extensive and fertile diluvial and alluvial plains—

majestic rivers—peaceful lakes, and every diversity of climate which the uncounted desires of man can crave. Here, too, is the pestilence-breeding marsh, the belching volcano, and convulsing earthquake,—all parts of this great whole, and all in wisdom regulated for man's ultimate good.

Nature, like the chemist, has her laboratory. The mountains are her refrigerators. It is by these she cools, condenses, and deposites the vapors which rise, under the influence of the sun, from the surface of the ocean; by these she manufactures the storm and arouses the whirlwind—racks into purity the stagnant air, and washes into freshness and life the arid plains beneath. Man needs dry land for other purposes than agriculture and manufacture. Life, and health, and locomotion, are more important than great cities or broad plantations;—hence God has not forgotten these in the economy of nature, but has diversified the earth with these secondary agents of his goodness, lakes and rivers, and variety of climate, to irrigate the soil, transport his produce, and connect, by links of mutual intercourse and dependence, every portion of the habitable earth.

Nothing can be more appalling than volcanoes and earthquakes. We are apt to consider the crust of earth, upon which we reside, as so solid and unchangeable a mass that it can neither be shaken or rent; but in many regions it is far from a state of repose. In the foci of volcanoes nothing can be more disastrously unstable than the crust of the earth. Within the life of a single generation the entire aspect of a neighborhood is changed—cities are engulphed in yawning fissures—hills levelled down and dislocated—mountains heaved up and crystalized—inhabitants buried in ruins, and the most appalling transformations effected in the whole region. Yet these have been, in the past developments of the earth, agents of the greatest good. All the useful and necessary variety of mountain and plain—hill and valley—river, and lake, and island, has been, in an unquestioned degree, the effect of their agency; and though their phenomena now, are not so evidently connected with beneficial results, we are at no loss to infer, from the past and the present combined, that they still play an important part among the great regulating and conservative powers of our globe.

But amidst so much to admire and to enjoy, is there nothing to deplore and avoid? Are all the successive creations, each of which God pronounced "*good,*" and and all of which He declared to be "*very good,*" still good? Are there no bitter waters mingled in this great fountain of general beneficence? Surely yes. Man has fallen, and his habitation is cursed; but it is cursed *for his sake.* The very sweat of our brow will one day be seen clearly to be a blessing, and the seeds of death which are around us and in us will germinate to the bringing forth of eternal life. Happy the man who can thus look upon nature, and trace in every arrangement a final cause of mercy! And should not all Christians so regard these manifold works of Him who in wisdom hath made them all, and be ready with the Psalmist to exclaim, "O Lord, the earth is full of thy riches! So is this great and wide sea, wherein are things creeping innumerable, both small and great beasts."

W. K. P.

www.ingramcontent.com/pod-product-compliance
Lightning Source LLC
LaVergne TN
LVHW021423110826
845150LV00007B/2064

* 9 7 8 1 4 2 5 5 0 8 0 3 6 *